YouTube Traffic Secrets: How to Drive Traffic to Your Links

Roy Hendershot

Published by Roy Hendershot, 2024.

While every precaution has been taken in the preparation of this book, the publisher assumes no responsibility for errors or omissions, or for damages resulting from the use of the information contained herein.

YOUTUBE TRAFFIC SECRETS: HOW TO DRIVE TRAFFIC TO YOUR LINKS

First edition. June 4, 2024.

Copyright © 2024 Roy Hendershot.

Written by Roy Hendershot.

Table of Contents

YouTube Traffic Secrets: How to Drive Traffic to Your Links 1

Chapter 1: The Power of YouTube 2

Chapter 2: Creating Irresistible Content 4

Chapter 3: Optimizing Your Video Titles 6

Chapter 4: Crafting Descriptions That Work 8

Chapter 5: The Magic of Thumbnails 10

Chapter 6: Interactive Elements - Cards and End Screens 12

Chapter 7: Engaging with Your Audience 14

Chapter 8: Promoting Your Videos 16

Chapter 9: Using Analytics to Improve 19

Chapter 10: Long-Term Strategies for Success 22

YouTube Traffic Secrets:

How to Drive Traffic to Your Links

Chapter 1: The Power of YouTube

YouTube isn't just for watching cute cat videos. It's a massive platform where millions of people watch, share, and create content every day. This makes YouTube a powerful tool for driving traffic to your links. Whether you're promoting a blog, a product, or a social media page, YouTube can help you reach a larger audience. Imagine you're a best-selling author who has unlocked the secrets of YouTube. People flock to your videos, and every link you share gets hundreds, even thousands, of clicks. Sounds amazing, right? It's possible, and this book will show you how.

Top YouTubers didn't start with millions of followers. They began with a plan, a bit of luck, and a lot of hard work. Their success stories show that anyone can make it big on YouTube. Take PewDiePie, for example. He started by making gaming videos in his bedroom. Now, he has millions of followers and a career many can only dream of. How did he do it? By understanding the platform and consistently creating engaging content.

YouTube's algorithm is a key player in this success. It loves engagement. The more people watch, like, and comment on your videos, the more the algorithm will promote your content. This means that getting people to interact with your videos is crucial. You can do this by creating content that people find interesting and want to share with their friends. The algorithm also favors consistency. Regular uploads help keep you on the algorithm's radar, giving your videos more chances to be seen.

Including links in your video descriptions can significantly boost your online presence. But first, you need to get people to see those links. This is where understanding YouTube's algorithm and creating engaging content comes in. By the end of this journey, you'll know how to use YouTube to its fullest potential. Ready to dive in? Let's get started!

One of the most exciting parts of YouTube is watching how creators grow over time. They didn't all start with fancy equipment or a big budget. Many began with just their creativity and determination. This is something you can do too. By following the steps in this book, you'll learn how to create content that attracts viewers and encourages them to click on your links.

Understanding YouTube's algorithm is like having a secret weapon. The algorithm decides which videos to promote based on engagement and relevance. To get the algorithm to favor your videos, you need to focus on creating content that keeps viewers watching and interacting. This means making videos that are not only interesting but also engaging.

Consistency is another key factor. The algorithm rewards regular uploads. This doesn't mean you have to upload every day, but having a consistent schedule helps. Whether it's once a week or twice a month, sticking to a schedule can help you stay on the algorithm's radar.

Links are a vital part of your YouTube strategy. Placing links in your video descriptions can drive traffic to your website, blog, or other social media platforms. But it's not just about placing links. It's about making those links irresistible to your viewers. This book will cover how to craft descriptions that not only inform but also entice viewers to click on your links.

Each chapter will dive deeper into specific strategies you need to succeed. From creating thumbnails that grab attention to using analytics to refine your approach, we've got you covered. Think of this book as your roadmap to YouTube success. Follow the steps, and you'll be driving traffic to your links in no time.

Success on YouTube doesn't happen overnight. It takes time, effort, and a willingness to learn and adapt. But with the right strategies, you can achieve your goals. So, buckle up and get ready for an exciting journey into the world of YouTube traffic secrets!

Chapter 2: Creating Irresistible Content

Creating irresistible content is the foundation of your YouTube success. Without engaging videos, it doesn't matter how many links you include; people won't click them if they don't find your content interesting. The first step is understanding your audience. Who are they? What do they like? What problems are they trying to solve? By answering these questions, you can tailor your content to meet their needs.

Let's say your audience loves cooking. You could create a series of videos showing how to make simple, delicious meals. But don't just stop at the recipes. Add your own twist. Maybe you have a quirky cooking style or funny commentary. These personal touches make your videos unique and more enjoyable to watch.

Once you've figured out what your audience wants, you need to pick the right content themes. These are the broad topics your videos will cover. For example, if you run a travel channel, your themes could include destination guides, travel tips, and cultural experiences. Sticking to a few core themes helps you stay focused and makes it easier for your audience to know what to expect from your channel.

Storytelling is a powerful tool in your content creation arsenal. Everyone loves a good story. It keeps people hooked and makes your content more memorable. Whether you're sharing a personal experience or explaining a complex topic, framing it as a story can make it more engaging. Remember, stories have a beginning, middle, and end. Use this structure to keep your viewers' attention from start to finish.

Video quality is also important. You don't need the most expensive equipment, but your videos should be clear and well-edited. Poor video or audio quality can distract from your message and turn viewers away. Invest in a decent camera and microphone, and learn some basic editing skills. There are plenty of free resources online that can help you improve your production quality.

Consistency in content creation is crucial. Uploading regularly helps you build an audience and keeps you in the algorithm's good graces. But consistency isn't just about frequency; it's also about maintaining a certain quality level. Your viewers should know what to expect from your videos. If one video is funny and light-hearted and the next is serious and somber, it can confuse your audience.

Engaging content also encourages viewers to interact. Ask questions, invite comments, and create calls to action. For example, you could end your videos by asking viewers to share their thoughts or suggestions in the comments. This not only increases engagement but also gives you valuable feedback on what your audience likes and dislikes.

Don't forget the importance of thumbnails. A good thumbnail can make a huge difference in whether someone clicks on your video. It should be eye-catching and accurately represent the content of your video. Think of it as a mini-poster for your video. Bright colors, clear text, and compelling images can help your thumbnail stand out.

Another key element is your video title. This is often the first thing viewers see, so it needs to grab their attention. Use relevant keywords and keep it concise. Avoid clickbait titles, as they can damage your credibility and frustrate viewers. Instead, focus on creating titles that are intriguing and informative.

Descriptions are also important. They provide context for your video and can include valuable links. Be sure to include keywords naturally and make your description as informative as possible. Don't forget to add a call to action, encouraging viewers to click on your links or watch more of your videos.

Now that we've covered the basics of creating irresistible content, let's move on to how you can optimize your videos to ensure they get the attention they deserve. By following these tips, you'll be well on your way to creating content that not only attracts viewers but also keeps them coming back for more.

Chapter 3: Optimizing Your Video Titles

Your video title is one of the first things viewers notice. It's like a book cover that gives a hint about the story inside. A good title can make the difference between someone clicking on your video or scrolling past it. To craft an effective title, you need to understand the role of keywords. Keywords are the terms people use when searching for content. Including relevant keywords in your title can help your video show up in search results.

But don't just stuff your title with keywords. It needs to be catchy and engaging too. Think of it as a headline in a newspaper. It should grab attention and make people want to learn more. For example, instead of a title like "Baking Cookies," you could use "How to Bake Perfect Chocolate Chip Cookies Every Time." This title is more specific and promises a valuable outcome.

Avoiding clickbait is important. Clickbait titles might get you clicks initially, but they can frustrate viewers if the content doesn't deliver what was promised. This can lead to high bounce rates, where viewers leave your video quickly, and can harm your channel's reputation. Aim for honesty and accuracy in your titles.

Testing and refining your titles can also make a big difference. If a title isn't performing well, don't be afraid to tweak it. YouTube allows you to edit video titles even after publishing. Experiment with different wordings and see what works best for your audience. Over time, you'll get a better sense of what types of titles attract the most views.

Using tools to find the best titles can save you time and effort. There are several online tools that can help you identify popular keywords and phrases related to your content. These tools analyze search trends and can give you insights into what people are looking for. Incorporate these keywords into your titles to improve your video's visibility.

It's also helpful to look at the titles of popular videos in your niche. What do they have in common? Are there certain phrases or structures that seem to work well?

While you don't want to copy exactly, you can draw inspiration from successful examples and adapt them to fit your own content.

Remember, your title should be concise. While it's tempting to include as much information as possible, shorter titles are often more effective. Aim for around 60 characters or less. This ensures that your entire title is visible in search results and on mobile devices.

Another strategy is to include numbers in your titles. Numbers can make your title more specific and intriguing. For example, "5 Easy Tips for Starting a Garden" is likely to attract more clicks than "Starting a Garden." Numbers give a clear indication of what viewers can expect and can make your content seem more actionable and valuable.

Action words can also make your titles more compelling. Words like "how to," "tips," "secrets," and "guide" suggest that your video will provide useful information. They create a sense of anticipation and encourage viewers to click and learn more.

Lastly, consider your target audience when crafting your titles. Think about what will appeal to them and what kind of language they use. Tailoring your titles to your audience's preferences can increase your chances of attracting the right viewers.

Optimizing your video titles is a crucial step in driving traffic to your links. By using relevant keywords, crafting engaging titles, and continually testing and refining your approach, you can increase your video's visibility and attract more viewers. Now, let's move on to the next chapter, where we'll discuss how to create effective video descriptions.

Chapter 4: Crafting Descriptions That Work

Your video description is a valuable piece of real estate on YouTube. It's not just a place to summarize your video; it's a powerful tool to drive traffic to your links. Crafting an effective description involves including relevant keywords, providing valuable information, and strategically placing your links.

What should you include in your video description? Start with a brief summary of your video. This helps viewers understand what to expect and can entice them to watch. Be clear and concise, highlighting the main points without giving everything away. Next, include relevant keywords naturally throughout your description. These keywords help YouTube understand what your video is about and can improve your search rankings.

Incorporating links in your descriptions is essential. These can be links to your website, blog, social media pages, or specific products you mention in the video. Place the most important links near the top of your description so they're easy to find. You can also include a call to action, encouraging viewers to click the links for more information or to take advantage of special offers.

Using timestamps and chapters in your descriptions can enhance the viewer experience. Timestamps allow viewers to jump to specific parts of your video, which can be especially useful for longer videos or tutorials. This not only helps keep viewers engaged but also shows that you value their time.

Keeping descriptions clear and concise is key. While it's important to include relevant information, avoid overwhelming viewers with too much text. Aim for a balance between providing enough detail to be informative and keeping it concise enough to maintain interest.

Let's talk about how to make your descriptions more engaging. One effective strategy is to tell a mini-story in your description. For example, if you're sharing a cooking tutorial, you could briefly describe why you love the recipe or a fun anecdote related to the dish. This personal touch can make your description more relatable and interesting.

Another tip is to use formatting to your advantage. Break up your text with short paragraphs, bullet points, or even emojis to make it more readable. A well-formatted description is easier to skim and can keep viewers engaged longer.

Don't forget to include links to your social media pages. Encouraging viewers to follow you on other platforms can help you build a stronger online presence and keep your audience engaged with your content outside of YouTube. You can also promote other videos or playlists in your descriptions, guiding viewers to more of your content.

It's important to regularly update your descriptions. As your channel grows and evolves, your descriptions should reflect these changes. Update old descriptions with new links, keywords, or information to keep them relevant and effective.

Engage with your audience in the comments section by referring to your description. For example, if someone asks a question that's answered in the video, you can reply with a link to the timestamped section in the description. This not only helps the viewer but also encourages others to check the description for useful information.

Using YouTube's default upload settings can save you time. You can create a template for your descriptions that includes standard information like social media links, your website, and a brief call to action. This ensures that all your videos have a consistent look and feel while allowing you to customize each description as needed.

Crafting effective descriptions is an ongoing process. As you learn more about your audience and what works best for your channel, you'll be able to refine your approach. By providing valuable information, strategically placing your links, and engaging with your viewers, you can make the most of your video descriptions and drive more traffic to your links.

Chapter 5: The Magic of Thumbnails

Thumbnails are the first thing viewers see when browsing YouTube. They play a crucial role in whether someone decides to click on your video or not. Think of thumbnails as the cover of a book; they need to be eye-catching and give a glimpse of what your video is about.

Why do thumbnails matter so much? Because they grab attention. In a sea of videos, a compelling thumbnail can make yours stand out. It should be visually appealing and relevant to the content of your video. Bright colors, clear images, and bold text can help your thumbnail catch the viewer's eye.

Designing eye-catching thumbnails involves a bit of creativity. Use high-quality images that are related to your video's topic. If your video is about cooking, a picture of the finished dish can be very appealing. Adding text to your thumbnail can also be effective, especially if it highlights a key point or question from your video.

Consistency in thumbnail style is important for building your brand. When viewers see a thumbnail, they should be able to recognize it as one of your videos. Use similar colors, fonts, and layouts across your thumbnails to create a cohesive look. This not only helps with brand recognition but also makes your channel look more professional.

Analyzing successful thumbnails can give you insights into what works. Look at the thumbnails of popular videos in your niche. What do they have in common? Are there certain colors or styles that seem to attract more views? While you don't want to copy exactly, you can take inspiration and adapt these elements to fit your own style.

Tools for creating thumbnails can make the process easier. There are several online tools and apps that allow you to design thumbnails quickly and easily. These tools often include templates, fonts, and other design elements that can help you create professional-looking thumbnails without needing advanced graphic design skills.

Thumbnails should accurately represent the content of your video. Avoid using misleading images or text just to get clicks. This can frustrate viewers and damage your credibility. Instead, focus on creating thumbnails that are both attractive and honest about what viewers can expect from your video.

Testing different thumbnails can help you find what works best. YouTube allows you to change your thumbnail even after a video is published. If a video isn't performing as well as you'd like, try switching to a different thumbnail and see if it makes a difference. Over time, you'll get a better sense of what types of thumbnails resonate with your audience.

Including your face in thumbnails can make them more personal and engaging. People are naturally drawn to faces, and showing your own can help create a connection with viewers. If your channel is more personality-driven, this can be especially effective.

Keep your thumbnails simple and uncluttered. Too much text or too many images can be overwhelming and make it hard to understand what your video is about at a glance. Focus on one or two key elements that clearly convey the main idea of your video.

Using contrasting colors can help your thumbnail stand out. Bright colors like red, yellow, and blue tend to catch the eye, especially when paired with contrasting backgrounds. Experiment with different color combinations to see what works best for your channel.

Remember, the goal of your thumbnail is to entice viewers to click on your video. By creating eye-catching, relevant, and consistent thumbnails, you can increase your chances of attracting more views and driving traffic to your links. Now, let's explore how to leverage YouTube's interactive elements like cards and end screens to further boost your channel's performance.

Chapter 6: Interactive Elements - Cards and End Screens

YouTube offers several interactive elements that can help you drive traffic to your links. Two of the most powerful tools are cards and end screens. These features allow you to add clickable links directly to your videos, making it easier for viewers to find your content and follow your links.

YouTube cards are interactive elements that can appear at any point during your video. They can link to other videos, playlists, channels, or external websites. Cards are a great way to keep viewers engaged and direct them to more of your content. For example, if you're talking about a specific topic and have another video that goes into more detail, you can add a card linking to that video.

Best practices for using cards include timing them strategically and making sure they enhance the viewer experience. Don't overload your video with too many cards, as this can be distracting. Instead, use them sparingly and at moments when they make the most sense, such as when you mention a related topic or offer additional resources.

Creating effective end screens is another way to boost engagement. End screens appear in the last 5-20 seconds of your video and can include links to other videos, playlists, channels, or external sites. They provide a final opportunity to keep viewers on your channel or direct them to your website.

When designing end screens, think about what you want viewers to do next. Do you want them to watch another video? Subscribe to your channel? Visit your website? Make it easy for them by providing clear, clickable options. You can use templates provided by YouTube or create your own custom end screens to match your brand.

Linking to playlists and channels can help you keep viewers on your channel longer. Playlists are a great way to group related videos together, making it easier for viewers to binge-watch your content. By linking to playlists in your cards and end screens, you can encourage viewers to watch more of your videos.

External links can be added to cards and end screens if you're part of the YouTube Partner Program. This allows you to direct viewers to your website, online store, or other external sites. Make sure these links are relevant and provide value to your viewers. For example, if you have a cooking channel, you could link to a page with the full recipe or to a product page for the cooking tools you used.

Analyzing the impact of cards and end screens can help you refine your strategy. YouTube Analytics provides data on how many people click on your cards and end screens, as well as how these elements affect viewer retention. Use this information to adjust your approach and improve the effectiveness of your interactive elements.

Customizing the timing and placement of your cards and end screens is important. Experiment with different times and positions to see what works best for your content. For example, placing a card right after you mention a related video can increase the chances of viewers clicking on it.

Remember to promote your interactive elements in your video. Mention your cards and end screens verbally to draw attention to them. For example, you could say, "Click the card in the top right corner to watch my other video on this topic," or "Check out the links on the end screen for more resources."

Using cards and end screens effectively can significantly enhance your YouTube strategy. By providing easy access to more of your content and relevant external links, you can keep viewers engaged and drive more traffic to your links. Now, let's explore how engaging with your audience can further boost your channel's performance.

Chapter 7: Engaging with Your Audience

Building a loyal audience involves more than just posting videos. It's about creating a community where viewers feel valued and heard. Engaging with your audience can increase viewer retention, boost your video's performance, and drive more traffic to your links.

Importance of viewer interaction cannot be overstated. Responding to comments shows that you value your viewers' input and can create a sense of community. It also encourages more people to comment, increasing your video's engagement metrics. Take the time to reply to comments, even if it's just a simple thank you. This small gesture can go a long way in building a loyal audience.

Conducting live streams is another great way to engage with your audience. Live streams allow you to interact with viewers in real-time, answer their questions, and get immediate feedback. This can help you build a deeper connection with your audience and make them feel more involved in your channel. Plus, live streams can be a lot of fun and give you a chance to show your personality.

Creating community posts can keep your audience engaged between video uploads. YouTube's Community tab allows you to post updates, polls, and even share behind-the-scenes content. This keeps your channel active and gives viewers more reasons to check back regularly. Use community posts to share sneak peeks of upcoming videos, ask for viewer input, or simply share something interesting.

Building a loyal subscriber base takes time and effort. One of the best ways to do this is by consistently delivering value to your viewers. Whether it's through entertaining content, informative tutorials, or engaging stories, make sure your videos provide something of worth to your audience. When viewers know they can rely on you for quality content, they're more likely to subscribe and stay engaged.

Encouraging viewers to like, comment, and share your videos can also boost engagement. A simple call to action at the end of your videos can remind viewers to take these actions. For example, you could say, "If you enjoyed this video, please give it a thumbs up and leave a comment below. Don't forget to share it with your friends!" These actions not only increase your video's engagement metrics but also help spread your content to a wider audience.

Engaging with your audience also involves listening to their feedback. Pay attention to the comments and messages you receive. What do viewers like about your videos? What do they think could be improved? Use this feedback to refine your content and make it more appealing to your audience. This not only helps you create better videos but also shows viewers that you value their opinions.

Collaborating with other creators can introduce your channel to new audiences and create a sense of community within your niche. Look for opportunities to collaborate with other YouTubers who share a similar audience. This could involve guest appearances, joint projects, or shout-outs. Collaborations can be a win-win situation, helping both channels grow and reach new viewers.

Hosting contests and giveaways can also boost engagement and drive traffic to your links. People love the chance to win something, and hosting a contest can generate excitement and encourage viewers to participate. Make sure to clearly outline the rules and how viewers can enter, and consider using your description to link to the contest details or entry form.

Engaging with your audience is an ongoing process. It's about building relationships and creating a sense of community. By responding to comments, hosting live streams, creating community posts, and listening to feedback, you can create a loyal audience that supports your channel and helps drive traffic to your links. Now, let's explore how promoting your videos through social media and other channels can further enhance your reach.

Chapter 8: Promoting Your Videos

Promoting your videos is essential for reaching a broader audience and driving traffic to your links. Social media platforms are powerful tools for spreading the word about your YouTube content. Sharing your videos on platforms like Facebook, Twitter, Instagram, and LinkedIn can help you reach people who might not find your videos through YouTube alone.

When sharing on social media, make sure to tailor your posts to fit each platform. For example, on Instagram, you might share a short clip or a behind-the-scenes photo with a link to the full video in your bio. On Twitter, you can use hashtags to reach a wider audience and tag relevant accounts. Each platform has its own style and audience, so adjust your approach accordingly.

Collaborating with other creators can introduce your channel to new audiences. Look for opportunities to work with YouTubers who have a similar target audience. Collaborations can take many forms, from guest appearances to joint projects. By working together, you can both benefit from each other's audiences and create content that's engaging and fun.

Utilizing email newsletters is another effective way to promote your videos. If you have a mailing list, send out regular updates with links to your latest videos. Include a brief summary of the video and why it's worth watching. Email newsletters can help you stay connected with your audience and remind them to check out your new content.

Engaging in online communities related to your niche can also help promote your videos. Participate in forums, Facebook groups, and other online spaces where your target audience hangs out. Share your expertise, answer questions, and when appropriate, share your videos. Be careful not to spam these communities with self-promotion; focus on providing value and building relationships.

Using ads to boost visibility can be a worthwhile investment. YouTube offers several advertising options, including TrueView ads, which allow viewers to choose whether or not to watch your ad. These ads can help you reach a larger audience and drive traffic to your videos. Facebook and Instagram also offer powerful advertising tools that can help you target specific demographics and interests.

Promoting your videos isn't just about getting more views; it's about attracting the right viewers. Focus on reaching people who are likely to be interested in your content and who will engage with your videos. This targeted approach can lead to more meaningful interactions and higher engagement rates.

Consistency in your promotional efforts is key. Regularly share your videos on social media, engage with your audience, and look for new opportunities to promote your content. Over time, these efforts can help you build a larger, more engaged audience.

Cross-promoting your videos on your other social media platforms can also drive traffic to your YouTube channel. For example, you can share a teaser of your latest video on Instagram with a link to the full video in your bio. Or, you could write a blog post related to your video topic and embed the video in the post. This not only promotes your video but also provides additional content for your followers.

Leveraging the power of hashtags can help your content get discovered on social media. Use relevant hashtags that are popular in your niche to increase the visibility of your posts. You can also create your own branded hashtags to encourage your audience to share your content and engage with your brand.

Analyzing the performance of your promotional efforts can help you refine your strategy. Use analytics tools provided by social media platforms and YouTube to track how your videos are performing. Look at metrics like views, engagement rates, and click-through rates to see what's working and what's not. Use this information to adjust your approach and improve your promotional efforts.

Promoting your videos through social media, collaborations, email newsletters, and online communities can help you reach a wider audience and drive traffic to your links. By being consistent and strategic in your promotional efforts, you can build a larger, more engaged audience. Now, let's explore how to use YouTube Analytics to improve your channel's performance and refine your strategy.

Chapter 9: Using Analytics to Improve

YouTube Analytics is a powerful tool that can provide valuable insights into your channel's performance. Understanding how to interpret and use this data can help you refine your strategy, improve your videos, and drive more traffic to your links. Let's dive into the key metrics and how to use them to your advantage.

Introduction to YouTube Analytics is essential for any serious content creator. YouTube provides a wealth of data on your channel's performance, including views, watch time, audience demographics, and engagement metrics. These insights can help you understand what's working and what needs improvement.

Understanding key metrics is the first step. Views are the total number of times your videos have been watched. Watch time measures how long viewers spend watching your videos, which is crucial for understanding engagement. Audience demographics provide information on the age, gender, and location of your viewers, helping you tailor your content to their preferences.

How to interpret your data involves looking at these metrics in context. For example, a high number of views is great, but if your watch time is low, it might indicate that viewers aren't finding your content engaging. Similarly, if your audience demographics show that most of your viewers are in a specific age group or location, you can create content that appeals more directly to them.

Adjusting your strategy based on analytics is key to improving your channel's performance. If you notice that certain types of videos get more views and engagement, consider making more content in that style. Conversely, if some videos aren't performing well, analyze why and think about how you can improve.

Setting goals and tracking progress can help you stay focused and motivated. Use your analytics data to set realistic goals for your channel, such as increasing your average watch time or gaining more subscribers. Track your progress over time and adjust your strategy as needed to stay on track.

Engagement metrics, such as likes, comments, and shares, provide valuable insights into how viewers are interacting with your content. High engagement rates can signal that your content resonates with your audience. Encourage viewers to like, comment, and share your videos to boost these metrics and increase your video's visibility.

Retention rates show how long viewers stay engaged with your videos. High retention rates indicate that your content is keeping viewers' attention. If you notice a drop-off point where viewers tend to leave, analyze that part of the video to see what might be causing it. This can help you create more engaging content in the future.

Traffic sources tell you where your viewers are coming from. This can include search results, suggested videos, external websites, and social media. Understanding your traffic sources can help you focus your promotional efforts and optimize your content for different platforms.

Using analytics to improve your thumbnails and titles is another effective strategy. If you notice that certain thumbnails or titles get more clicks, try to identify what makes them stand out. Use this information to create more compelling thumbnails and titles for future videos.

Analyzing audience behavior can provide deeper insights into how viewers interact with your content. Look at metrics like average view duration, click-through rates, and the number of returning viewers. This can help you understand what keeps viewers coming back and how to create content that meets their needs.

Regularly reviewing your analytics data can help you stay on top of your channel's performance and make informed decisions. Set aside time each week or month to review your analytics and make any necessary adjustments to your strategy.

Using YouTube Analytics to refine your strategy is an ongoing process. As you learn more about your audience and what works for your channel, you'll be able to create more effective content and drive more traffic to your links. Now, let's explore how to implement paid promotion to boost your video's visibility and reach a larger audience.

Chapter 10: Long-Term Strategies for Success

Building a successful YouTube channel is a long-term endeavor. It requires consistency, creativity, and a willingness to adapt. In this chapter, we'll explore strategies for maintaining and growing your channel over time, ensuring you continue to drive traffic to your links and achieve your goals.

Building a brand on YouTube is essential for long-term success. Your brand is more than just your content; it's your identity on the platform. It includes your channel's visual style, the tone of your videos, and the way you interact with your audience. A strong brand helps you stand out and makes your channel more recognizable.

Diversifying your content can keep your channel fresh and attract a broader audience. While it's important to stay true to your core themes, experimenting with different types of videos can help you discover new opportunities and keep your viewers engaged. For example, if you have a cooking channel, you might try adding travel vlogs that explore culinary traditions around the world.

Monetizing your channel can provide additional income and resources to invest back into your content. YouTube offers several monetization options, including ads, channel memberships, and Super Chat. Additionally, you can explore sponsorships, merchandise, and affiliate marketing. Diversifying your revenue streams can help you sustain your channel financially and continue creating high-quality content.

Staying updated with trends is crucial in the fast-paced world of YouTube. Trends can provide inspiration for new content and help you stay relevant. Keep an eye on what's popular in your niche and be ready to adapt. However, it's important to balance following trends with maintaining your unique voice and style.

Maintaining motivation and avoiding burnout is essential for long-term success. Creating content regularly can be demanding, and it's easy to feel overwhelmed. Find ways to stay inspired, such as collaborating with other creators, taking breaks when needed, and setting achievable goals. Remember why you started your channel and keep that passion alive.

Building a community around your channel can create a loyal audience that supports your long-term success. Engage with your viewers, encourage them to share your content, and create opportunities for them to interact with each other. A strong community can provide valuable feedback, support your channel, and help you grow.

Investing in your skills and equipment can enhance the quality of your content and help you stay competitive. Consider taking courses in video production, editing, or marketing to improve your skills. Upgrading your equipment, such as cameras, microphones, and editing software, can also make a noticeable difference in your video's quality.

Setting long-term goals can help you stay focused and measure your progress. Think about where you want your channel to be in one year, five years, or even ten years. Set specific, measurable goals and create a plan to achieve them. Regularly review your goals and adjust your strategy as needed to stay on track.

Balancing content creation with promotion is key to sustaining your channel's growth. While creating high-quality videos is important, promoting your content is equally crucial. Find a balance that works for you, ensuring you're dedicating enough time to both creating and promoting your videos.

Learning from your mistakes and successes can help you refine your approach. Analyze what has worked well for your channel and what hasn't. Use this information to make informed decisions and continuously improve your content and strategy.

Staying connected with your audience is essential for long-term success. Regularly engage with your viewers, listen to their feedback, and make them feel valued. Building strong relationships with your audience can create a loyal fan base that supports your channel and helps you grow.

Continuously evolving and adapting is key to staying relevant on YouTube. The platform and its audience are constantly changing, so it's important to stay flexible and open to new ideas. Embrace change and use it as an opportunity to innovate and improve your content.

Focusing on your unique strengths can set your channel apart. Identify what makes your content special and highlight these qualities in your videos. Whether it's your storytelling ability, your expertise in a particular area, or your engaging personality, leveraging your strengths can help you stand out in a crowded field.

Celebrating your achievements and milestones can keep you motivated and connected with your audience. Whether it's reaching a subscriber milestone, receiving positive feedback, or completing a challenging project, take the time to acknowledge and celebrate your successes.

Long-term success on YouTube requires a combination of consistency, creativity, and strategic planning. By building a strong brand, diversifying your content, staying updated with trends, and maintaining a healthy balance between creation and promotion, you can sustain your channel's growth and continue driving traffic to your links. Remember, the journey is just as important as the destination. Enjoy the process, stay true to yourself, and keep creating content that you and your audience love.

www.ingramcontent.com/pod-product-compliance
Lightning Source LLC
Chambersburg PA
CBHW050037230526
45470CB00003B/1323